NOV. 04

Reducing Gun Violence:
The St. Louis Consent-to-Search Program

Acknowledgments

The authors gratefully acknowledge the assistance of many individuals who made this research possible and helped to improve it, especially: Sgt. Simon Risk (ret.), Capt. Joe Richardson, Sgt. Terry Sloan, Sgt. Bob Heimberger, Sgt. Tom Malacek, and Maj. Lawrence O'Toole from the St. Louis Metropolitan Police Department; and George Burruss of Southern Illinois University–Carbondale, Bruce Jacobs of the University of Texas–Dallas, Steve Mastrofski of George Mason University, and Phil Cook of Duke University. Lois Felson Mock was the NIJ Program Manager for this grant. Her oversight was integral to the successful completion of this project.

Findings and conclusions of the research reported here are those of the authors and do not reflect the official position or policies of the U.S. Department of Justice.

This research was sponsored by the National Institute of Justice, U.S. Department of Justice, under grant number 95–IJ–CX–0067.

NCJ 191332

U.S. Department of Justice
Office of Justice Programs

810 Seventh Street N.W.

Washington, DC 20531

John Ashcroft
Attorney General

Deborah J. Daniels
Assistant Attorney General

Sarah V. Hart
Director, National Institute of Justice

This and other publications and products
of the National Institute of Justice can be
found at:

National Institute of Justice
www.ojp.usdoj.gov/nij

Office of Justice Programs
Partnerships for Safer Communities
www.ojp.usdoj.gov

Foreword

This Research Report is part of the National Institute of Justice's (NIJ's) Reducing Gun Violence publication series. Each report in the series describes the implementation and effects of an individual, NIJ-funded, local-level program designed to reduce firearm-related violence in a particular U.S. city. Some studies received cofunding from the U.S. Department of Justice's Office of Community Oriented Policing Services; one also received funding from the Centers for Disease Control and Prevention.

Each report in the series describes in detail the problem targeted; the program designed to address it; the problems confronted in designing, implementing, and evaluating the effort; and the strategies adopted in responding to any obstacles encountered. Both successes and failures are discussed, and recommendations are made for future programs.

While the series includes impact evaluation components, it primarily highlights implementation problems and issues that arose in designing, conducting, and assessing the respective programs.

The Research Reports should be of particular value to anyone interested in adopting a strategic, data-driven, problem-solving approach to reducing gun violence and other crime and disorder problems in communities.

The series reports on firearm violence reduction programs in Boston, Indianapolis, St. Louis, Los Angeles, Atlanta, and Detroit.

Contents

Scott H. Decker and Richard Rosenfeld

An Innovative Gun Recovery Program

This report is based on "From Problem Solving to Crime Suppression to Community Mobilization: An Evaluation of the St. Louis Consent-to-Search Program," final report by the authors to the National Institute of Justice, 2001, available at http://www.ncjrs.org/pdffiles1/nij/grants/188291.pdf.

About the Authors

Scott H. Decker, Ph.D., is Curator's Professor of Criminology and Criminal Justice at the University of Missouri–St. Louis. Richard Rosenfeld, Ph.D., is professor and chair of the Criminology and Criminal Justice Department at the University of Missouri–St. Louis.

In 1994, facing an epidemic of violent crime, St. Louis instituted an innovative program to reduce its alarmingly high gun violence rates among youths. The idea for the program came from a community meeting of residents and police. During the meeting a woman complained about a house where teenagers were known to possess guns. When police arrived, the children ran into the house. Officers at the meeting told the woman there was nothing they could do because there was no legal way to get in and not enough information to obtain a search warrant. She then asked a single question that changed everything: "Why don't you just knock on the door and ask that mother if you can search the house?"

The officers realized that the woman was right. Thus, the Consent-to-Search program was born.[1]

The program involved police knocking on doors in high-crime areas and asking parents of high-risk youths for permission to search their homes for guns that their children might have hidden. Any guns found were confiscated, with no followup prosecution. Parents and young people who requested help were referred to agencies or community-based groups that offered appropriate services.

Program success and shifts

The Consent-to-Search program emerged during the national epidemic of youth violence in the late 1980s and early 1990s.[2] (See "Homicides and Other Violent Crime in St. Louis.") In its first year, police confiscated 402 guns from juveniles. They encountered remarkable cooperation within the communities that were most affected by gun violence.

The program won national recognition. It was covered widely in the media, nominated for a prestigious award, and reviewed by a congressional committee. In October 1995, the National Institute of Justice funded an evaluation of the program to assess its effectiveness and determine its applicability to other cities.

As a strategic problem-solving approach to reducing gun violence by getting guns out of the hands of juveniles, Consent-to-Search appeared destined to become a model community policing initiative.

This situation changed abruptly in December 1995, when the chief of police who had established Consent-to-Search stepped down. Over the next several years, local government decisions resulted in the program starting and stopping twice—each time with a different format and set of objectives. The program was terminated in August 1999.

Lessons learned

The Consent-to-Search story offers valuable insights about

HOMICIDES AND OTHER VIOLENT CRIME IN ST. LOUIS

After falling for several years, national homicide rates of persons between 14 and 24 years old escalated rapidly after 1985, peaking in 1993. By the early 1990s, guns were readily available to children in many cities through street corner markets.[a]

The homicide increase in St. Louis during the late 1980s and early 1990s[b] was concentrated among African-American adolescents and young adults. By the early 1990s, the city's homicide rate reached 380 per 100,000 for black males ages 15–19 and an astonishing 600 per 100,000 for black males ages 20–24. More than 97 percent of these deaths involved firearms.[c]

The levels of criminal violence have been sharply higher in St. Louis than in most other cities, although the demographic patterns of risk are quite similar to other cities.[d] Changes in St. Louis homicide rates over the past 30 years correspond closely with national rates,[e] which suggests that interventions shown to be effective in St. Louis might be promising candidates for broader adoption.

Notes

a. American Psychological Association, *Violence and Youth: Psychology's Response: Volume I: Summary Report of the American Psychological Association Commission on Violence and Youth,* Washington, DC: 1993.

b. Cook, P.J., and J.H. Laub, "The Unprecedented Epidemic in Youth Violence," in *Youth Violence,* vol. 24 of *Crime and Justice: A Review of Research,* ed. M. Tonry and M.H. Moore, Chicago: University of Chicago Press, 1998.

c. Rosenfeld, R., and S. Decker, "Consent to Search and Seize: Evaluating an Innovative Youth Firearm Suppression Program," *Law and Contemporary Problems* 59 (1996): 197–220 (hereinafter "Consent to Search and Seize").

d. See Jones, M., and B. Krisberg, *Image and Reality: Juvenile Crime, Youth Violence, and Public Policy,* Washington, DC: National Council on Crime and Delinquency, 1994. Also see Snyder, H., and M. Sickmund, *Juvenile Offenders and Victims: A Focus on Violence, A Statistics Summary,* Washington, DC: U.S. Department of Justice, 1995, NCJ 153570.

e. Rosenfeld and Decker, "Consent to Search and Seize."

reducing youth gun violence. These insights are especially significant for community policing as it tries to gain a toehold in the traditional culture of policing and institutional responses to crime.

The original Consent-to-Search program was based on the standard community policing approach of responding to a problem identified by citizens. By drawing citizens into the process of identifying and confiscating illegal firearms, officers relied on community expertise—a central tenet of problem-solving policing.[3] For example, officers in the first phase of the program believed that its success depended on scrupulous adherence to the promise of no prosecution. They were willing to ignore evidence of all but the most serious crimes in return for access to the homes of juveniles with firearms. This view—that arrest opportunities are worth trading for the chance to get guns out of kids' hands—is essential to this type of intervention's success.

Consent-to-Search can be viewed as a variant of both the aggressive order maintenance and targeted deterrence strategies.[4] The intervention sent a signal that juvenile firearm possession poses great risks, threatens public order, and will not be tolerated by the police or the community. The success of such an effort depends heavily on the quality of the interaction between the community and law enforcement.

But a central theme of the story is the difficulty of sustaining law enforcement innovations in the face of strong organizational resistance and weak external support. It is not enough to have a good idea for an intervention, or even to have a good working intervention. Problem-solving initiatives must build support at all levels within the police department. They must also be anchored within the community, by design and through partnerships and routine contact. Programs that do not establish these elements are vulnerable to changes in leadership, policy, or other influences that may counteract or shut down the intervention.

Communities seeking interventions to reduce gun violence, especially among youths, might consider using consent searches as part of a comprehensive gun recovery strategy. (See "Gun Recovery Strategies—Consent-to-Search in Context.")

...a central theme of the story is the difficulty of sustaining law enforcement innovations in the face of strong organizational resistance and weak external support.

GUN RECOVERY STRATEGIES—CONSENT-TO-SEARCH IN CONTEXT

Police use seven tactics to recover firearms and potentially reduce gun violence:

- Search warrants
- Pedestrian stops
- Arrests
- Gun buybacks
- Traffic stops
- Gun turn-in campaigns
- Consent searches

As each tactic has something to contribute to illegal firearm recovery, the police should employ a mix of complementary tactics to be effective in reducing illegal firearm use. Communities considering gun violence reduction strategies may want to carefully balance factors of risk, outcome, and costs (see exhibit 1).

Risk. A gun recovery intervention should first consider the level of risk for each strategy. For example, search warrants and arrests generally identify high-risk offenders who pose a danger to officers. Because consent searches target individuals considered to be at risk for involvement in crime, either as victims or offenders, they are likely to have a greater crime-reduction payoff than pedestrian or traffic stops—while posing less risk for police.

Probability of gun seizure. A second criterion for choosing a gun recovery intervention is the probability that a gun will be found. Those efforts most likely to yield guns—search warrants and gun buybacks—are the most dangerous and least dangerous tactics, respectively. Although traffic and pedestrian stops are deemed the least likely to get guns, they account for the majority of gun seizures because of the sheer volume of these stops—literally thousands per year.[a]

Search warrants, gun buybacks, and gun turn-in campaigns have a high yield in firearms but account for only a fraction of the guns recovered by the police. Guns recovered through buybacks and turn-in campaigns are the least likely to have been involved in crime.

Crime reduction and social costs. Another consideration is whether the removal of guns through a given tactic or set of tactics results in a net reduction in crime. Search warrants and arrests usually are executed because an offense has occurred or is imminent; therefore, they are most likely to reduce criminal activity in the near term. All of the other tactics, including consent searches, are less likely to identify an individual involved in crime during gun seizure or in the near future.

Tactics that have an immediate effect on crime have an intuitive appeal. Search warrants, arrests, and some traffic and pedestrian stops have this potential if officers are trained to look for firearms.[b] But traffic and pedestrian stops can have substantial social implications. A major complaint about U.S. law enforcement is the alleged use of racial profiling to stop minorities in proportions far greater than their representation in the population. Thus, traffic and pedestrian stops generate distrust of the police for many Americans.

Gun Recovery Strategies (continued)

Search warrants, arrests, and consent searches exact more moderate social costs because, although these tactics are invasive, the perceived crime-control benefits offset their intrusiveness. When done in close partnership with the community, consent searches may actually increase police-citizen cooperation and therefore have a low social cost.

Collaboration. A final dimension for comparing these strategies is whether a collaborative partner is needed. Activities that rely on collaboration between police and the community—such as consent searches—are more difficult to execute than those that the police can perform themselves. Nonetheless, consent searches based on police-citizen collaboration have proved to be an effective, relatively low-risk tactic to recover illegal firearms from juveniles.

Exhibit 1. Impact of gun recovery tactics

	Level of risk from subject	Probability of getting a gun	Difficulty of getting a gun	Crime reduction impact	Cost ($)	Social cost	Collaboration required
Search warrants	High	High	High	High	High	Medium	No
Arrests	High	Medium	Medium	High	Medium	Medium	No
Traffic stops	Medium/Low	Low	Low	Low	Low	Medium/High	No
Pedestrian stops	High	Low	Low	Low	Low	High	No
Consent searches	Medium/Low	Medium	Medium	Medium	Medium	Low	Yes
Gun buybacks	Low	High	Low	Low	Medium	Low	Yes
Gun turn-in campaigns	Low	High	Low	Low	Low	Low	No

Notes

a. See Burruss, G.W., and S.H. Decker, "Gun Violence and Police Problem Solving: A Research Note Examining Alternative Data Sources," *Journal of Criminal Justice* 30(6) (Nov./Dec. 2002): 567–574.

b. See Sherman, L., J. Shaw, and D. Rogan, *The Kansas City Gun Experiment*, Research in Brief, Washington, DC: U.S. Department of Justice, National Institute of Justice, 1995, NCJ 150855.

Program Phases and Results

In its earliest stage, Consent-to-Search was a police problem-solving tool directed at one of St. Louis's most serious crime problems. In its later stages, however, the program fundamentally changed. To evaluate the program in the face of the major changes that occurred in 1996 and 1998, researchers divided it into three phases that correspond to the changes in operational philosophy and approach used by police (see exhibit 2.) This made it easier to identify the effects of program changes. (See exhibit 3 for a timeline depicting pivotal events and program changes.)

Phase I—Problem Solving/Aggressive Order Maintenance

The St. Louis Consent-to-Search program in Phase I

Exhibit 2. **St. Louis Consent-to-Search program phases**

	Phase I *Problem Solving/ Aggressive Order Maintenance*	Phase II *Crime Control/ Suppression*	Phase III *Targeted Intervention/ Attempted Community Mobilization*
Program goals and methods			
Orientation	▪ Problem solving ▪ Aggressive order maintenance	▪ Crime control ▪ Suppression	▪ Community policing ▪ Community mobilization
Tools	▪ Consent searches	▪ Search warrants ▪ Arrests	▪ Consent searches ▪ Referrals
Sources of search target information	▪ Community meetings	▪ Police ▪ Intelligence	▪ Police ▪ Police Information Record System ▪ Gang unit ▪ Intelligence
Objectives	▪ Respond to citizens' concerns ▪ Seize weapons from juveniles ▪ Notify parents ▪ Refer parents to assistance	▪ Make arrests ▪ Seize weapons ▪ Gain intelligence ▪ Serve warrants	▪ Seize weapons ▪ Make referrals ▪ Involve a community partner ▪ Notify parents
Program process	▪ Home visits ▪ Consent requests	▪ Warrants	▪ Home visits ▪ Consent requests

7

combined two proven aspects of community policing: problem solving and aggressive order maintenance. In its first full year of operation, the program enjoyed spectacular success, especially in three areas: citizen cooperation, the targeting of locations that were likely to yield guns, and the confiscation of firearms. Of citizens who were approached, 98 percent consented to a search. This degree of cooperation is quite remarkable, given the historic pattern of distrust between the police and the black community in St. Louis.[5]

Cases in this phase were initiated mostly by citizens who identified homes to search.

The program was operated by the Mobile Reserve unit, a squad without a specific geographic assignment that responds to pockets of crime and violence throughout the city. Training was conducted within the unit. Officers involved in this phase attributed its early success to its low-key approach.[6] Two officers and a Mobile Reserve sergeant visited the residence in question, spoke with an adult resident, and requested permission to search the home for illegal weapons.

In 1994, the Mobile Reserve unit conducted between 5 and 30 searches each night the program was in operation. Guns were found in half of

Exhibit 3. **St. Louis Consent-to-Search program timeline**

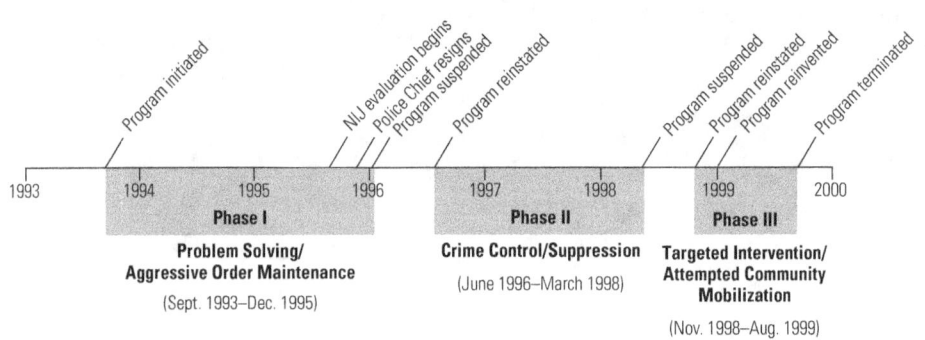

the homes searched; an average of three guns were seized per household. Anecdotal evidence indicated strong support for the program among adults in neighborhoods that experienced high levels of gun violence. One parent even offered to sign several predated forms so that the police could return at any time; another wanted to give police a key to her house so they could search while she was at work.

An innovative feature of the program was the use of a "Consent to Search and Seize" form to secure legal access to the residence (see exhibit 4). Residents were assured that the sole purpose was to confiscate illegal firearms possessed by juveniles and that by providing written consent to search, they would not be charged with illegal possession of a firearm.

Phase II—Crime Control/Suppression

One month after the police chief who founded the Consent-to-Search program resigned, his successor suspended the program. In early 1996, the lead evaluator met with the new commander of the division housing the Mobile Reserve unit. The

commander was unaware of the program's accomplishments; researchers showed him a newspaper article to convince him. He agreed to resume the program, but only in a new form. The Phase II program had a different set of objectives and procedures. The primary goal of consent searches changed from seizing guns to arresting offenders.

The changes were drastic: the department abandoned the problem-solving approach of removing weapons from juveniles through consent in favor of traditional crime control and suppression. Arrests, search warrants, and intelligence gathering replaced the original goals of consent, no arrests, and referrals for services.

Consent searches were relegated to a marginal role as more aggressive tactics—especially search warrants—received top priority. The new lieutenant in charge of the Mobile Reserve unit explained the shift in philosophy: "Why only get a gun with a consent search, when you can get a gun and a criminal with an arrest or search warrant?"

The program received little support from members of the newly constituted Mobile Reserve unit. No training was provided; many in the unit

Exhibit 4. **The Consent to Search and Seize form**

**ST. LOUIS METROPOLITAN POLICE DEPARTMENT
MOBILE RESERVE SECTION
FIREARM SUPPRESSION PROGRAM**

CONSENT TO SEARCH AND SEIZE

Police Officers of the Mobile Reserve Section are currently engaged in a Firearm Suppression Program. The purpose of this Firearm Suppression Program is to locate and recover illegal and/or unregistered firearms. As part of this program said officers agree that should any illegal or unregistered firearms be located in the residence the person authorizing the search of the premises will not be charged with illegal possession of a firearm.

Having authority to authorize a search of the premises, do hereby grant officers of the St. Louis Metropolitan Police Department permission to search and remove any illegal and/or unregistered firearms.

POLICE OFFICER _____ SIGNATURE _____

DATE _____ OF _____
                                  (Address)

FIREARMS SEIZED:

_____

_____

MPD FORM MobReserve-1 (2/95)

were unaware of the program. The pledge of no prosecution was removed from the consent-to-search form. After 9 months of warranted searches that yielded relatively few guns, the program was discontinued, although it was not officially terminated until 12 months later.

Phase III—Targeted Intervention/Attempted Community Mobilization

In January 1999, the Consent-to-Search program was reestablished as a result of support from the U.S. Attorney's Office,[7] the availability of Federal funding,[8] and continued national and local attention to youth firearm violence, which kept pressure on the police department to do something about guns in the hands of juveniles.

Phase III operated differently from the earlier phases. Moved from Mobile Reserve to the Intelligence unit, the program was conducted on an overtime basis. Officers were trained and program activities were documented. The original consent-to-search form with promise of no prosecution was restored. Participating officers were chosen because they had served in Phase I and were committed to the policy, elements not present in Phase II. This link to Phase I lent credibility to the new initiative.

A hallmark of Phase I was its reliance on community input as a major source of target addresses for consent searches. In contrast, Phase III relied primarily on internal police data sources to select juveniles who had been arrested or mentioned in a field incident report.

Another new element in Phase III was a formal partnership with a coalition of African-American churches called the African-American Churches in Dialogue. This group was formed to present a unified voice and leadership regarding social issues affecting the black community in St. Louis. The police requested the group's help with referrals from consent searches, and the group also agreed to counsel parents and youths. The officers were relieved to have somewhere to refer distraught or desperate parents.

Program results

Gaps in data resulting from programmatic changes and operational lapses constrained the evaluators' ability to measure overall program impact. However, program changes and some outcomes were documented.

Phase I. The comparative success of the Phase I approach as a means of gaining parental consent and seizing illegal guns from juveniles is evident from the nearly total rate of parental compliance and the high number of guns seized (see exhibit 5).

Phase II. Guns seized in this phase were largely from search warrants and arrests, as consent searches were not used. During the approximately 9 operational months of Phase II, only 6 percent as many guns were recovered as during the 12 operational months of Phase I.

Phase III. Despite some favorable features, Phase III did not match the achievements of Phase I. Granting of consent fell by nearly 50 percent, and the number of guns seized remained nearly 90 percent below Phase I levels. This phase was heavily police driven, which may account for the much lower level of compliance by parents or guardians than in Phase I. As the police assumed greater responsibility for determining where to search, relying on neighborhood sources less, they met with more refusals and recovered significantly fewer guns from youths.[9]

Another factor that also could have affected the number of illegal firearms seized in Phase III is that overall levels of youth firearm violence had fallen in St. Louis and other large cities during that period (1998–99). There may have been fewer illegal firearms in the community.

Exhibit 5. **St. Louis Consent-to-Search program results**

	Phase I	**Phase II**	**Phase III**
Consent given	98%	Not applicable	42%
Hit rate (percent of searches netting a gun)	50%	Not applicable	<25%
Program duration	18 months	9 months	9 months
Guns seized	510	31	29
Community partner	Parents and neighbors	None	Clergy

Evaluating a Changing Program

The Consent-to-Search program evaluation suffered from implementation lapses and changes in program design and execution. Phase I records were lost;[10] to evaluate that phase, researchers interviewed police about their recollections and relied on the public record. Phase II data sources were activity logs, ride-alongs, observations, and interviews. Phase III sources were police records, reports, interviews, and ride-alongs.

Researchers tried unsuccessfully to convince the police to concentrate on a few high-crime neighborhoods, employing similar neighborhoods as controls. Otherwise, the team argued, the impact of the program on firearm violence would be diluted and difficult to measure. However, the police preferred a problem-solving approach that focused on high-risk youths rather than high-risk areas.[11] This made an outcome evaluation infeasible.

Process evaluation obstacles

Ideally, a process evaluation would identify the attributes of individuals, the program components, and the community characteristics associated with a high level of citizen compliance with police search requests and with a high ratio of firearm confiscations to searches. But researchers faced major challenges in collecting such process data because of the changing nature of the program. For example,

- Targets of searches were determined by different sources in each phase and thus were not comparable throughout the program phases.

- Degree of compliance could not be a process measure since searches in Phase II were warrant searches, not consent searches.

- Phase III introduced a community partnership element not present in the other two phases.

Impact evaluation obstacles

To measure program impact, a model outcome evaluation of the Consent-to-Search program would have pursued three objectives:

■ Determine whether the program reduced youth firearm possession, i.e., did youths rearm after their guns were confiscated?

■ Determine whether confiscation of guns threatened the personal security of young people, i.e., did they believe that without a gun they were more at risk to become victims of violence?

■ Measure the program's effect on the level of community safety, including firearms crime and victimization in neighborhoods.

Ideally, juveniles whose homes were searched would have been contacted and interviewed regarding their rearming and sense of personal security. Because evaluators could not determine the effectiveness of Consent-to-Search in meeting the first two objectives, they could not evaluate the program's impact on community safety.

Implementation Problems

Despite the intuitive sense Consent-to-Search made for a city with very high rates of youth violence, the program could not be sustained because of fundamental deficiencies in how it was implemented and maintained. Attempts in Phase III to correct some of these problems were insufficient, although Phase III did raise awareness of the program within the department and among other law enforcement and city agencies.

Why the program ended

The Consent-to-Search program's demise is rooted in six broad areas.

Uncommitted leadership. A distinctive organizational culture is required to encourage and sustain favorable attitudes about problem-solving initiatives among police officers. Strong leadership is especially needed. After the first chief left, the St. Louis Police Department had no organizational commitment to either problem solving or community policing. The prevailing departmental philosophy from early 1996 into 1998 was that consent searches were ineffective and too soft on offenders. Departmental leadership placed a higher priority on taking offenders rather than guns off the streets.

Officer resistance. The toughest impediment to implementing and sustaining problem-solving initiatives is officer resistance. Even in police departments that encourage problem-solving strategies, organizational support for an intervention such as Consent-to-Search can be precarious. For example, an ongoing issue throughout the program was whether it constituted "real police work." Some officers viewed the program as a community relations exercise with little impact on crime.

Program isolation. Problem-solving or community policing initiatives are often handled by a single police unit or division, as opposed to across the department. Subunit autonomy helps to insulate officers from the traditional norms and procedures of "real police work," i.e., making arrests, investigating crimes, pursuing offenders.[12] The drawback is that subunit autonomy can lead to unit isolation, which works against integrating innovations into the department's mainstream. In this case, the Mobile Reserve unit's isolation prevented other captains and lieutenants from accepting program goals and methods.

Lack of training. Without a formal training manual, program description, and documentation of past achievements, an innovation cannot diffuse throughout the department. What training existed was limited to the unit, which insulated the program from routine inservice training and adoption by the department as a whole.

Absence of followup. The final blow to Consent-to-Search was the apparent inability of the Phase III community partner (the African-American Churches in Dialogue) to follow up on referrals received from the police. The evaluation team was unable to document a single case of followup. This breakdown created a dilemma for some officers and fueled others' cynicism about police involvement in this type of intervention.

Lack of institutional memory. The St. Louis Police Department kept few records of Consent-to-Search until the program's last year. No entries were made in the confiscated firearms logs regarding method of confiscation. Such records would have documented the effectiveness of consent searches compared with other confiscation methods. In the absence of documentation, officers could legitimately question the veracity of the program's early reputation for success. As noted previously, failure to establish outcome measures made program evaluation difficult, if not impossible.

A unique legacy

Where in the inventory of innovations is the Consent-to-Search program best situated? Perhaps the best known police problem-solving partnership—and a good benchmark—is the Boston Gun Project's Operation Ceasefire program.[13] The success of that intervention hinged on the broad array of constituents who embraced the program, the continuous review of data to assess program progress, and the close linking of the program to review findings. These Operation Ceasefire characteristics were absent from Consent-to-Search.

However, the program's extraordinary achievements in Phase I give it a unique status among gun violence interventions. Coupling this success with the program's failures makes Consent-to-Search a potent example of the difficulties in program implementation that policymakers and practitioners must bear in mind. Even the most successful program will face challenges.

Implications for Community Policing

Problem-solving policing works best if police take their cues from the community. When Consent-to-Search lost that connection, gun seizure levels fell substantially below the levels achieved in Phase I when the community was involved. It is not unusual for a police department to return to the philosophy and tactics that were the backbone of law enforcement activity for most of the 20th century. Such a reversion is more likely if an innovation was never routinely implemented or institutionalized.

Past research shows that failure to develop a constituency, lack of support from community residents, and officer resistance have been the main impediments to community policing efforts.[14] The St. Louis Consent-to-Search program's experience, it seems, was not unique in this regard. In Phase I, these impediments were absent and the program enjoyed considerable success. However, each of these three impediments played a role in the program's difficulties in Phases II and III.

Absence of a constituency

Probably the greatest reason for Consent-to-Search's overall failure was the program's lack of a constituency, either internally within the police department or externally among city or community leadership or the citizenry.

Internal. Problem-solving innovations cannot survive without internal proponents who have sufficient prestige and influence to protect them from internal and external challenges. For the Consent-to-Search program to have survived the first police chief's resignation, supporters within the department's leadership and rank-and-file officers would have been necessary. None came forward until Phase III.

Community and parental. As critical as internal constituencies are, external constituencies are even more important. Participation by community groups willing to work with law enforcement is difficult to achieve in high-crime communities where

The presence of the police on their doorsteps seemed to indicate or reinforce to many parents that a problem existed and that they should cooperate.

tension between residents and police can run high.

Phase I's success in gaining consent to enter a home may have been due to a program emphasis on officer civility, but it also may reflect parental concern for their children's safety and well-being—in effect a parental constituency. The presence of the police on their doorsteps seemed to indicate or reinforce to many parents that a problem existed and that they should cooperate. Phase I was the only phase to exploit this intangible factor. Phase II ignored this element, and Phase III restored it only partially.

Lack of community support

Phase I achieved significant community cooperation in providing information about homes to target for searches; however, these sources were not recruited as active participants—as an advisory board or support group, for example. Had neighborhood groups been strongly committed to the program, it might not have been suspended and redesigned. Isolation of the program in a small police unit that was not neighborhood based also worked against

developing a community constituency. Such constituencies are best developed through sustained contact between officers and citizens.

Phase II made little to no effort to involve the community.

During Phase III, the community partner did not follow up on police referrals for services. This unanticipated development reveals the difficulties in forging effective partnerships between law enforcement and community organizations during problem-solving experiments. What went wrong is unclear. One implication is the need to review how community partnerships function in problem-solving initiatives and whether the partners have the requisite skills and commitment.

Overcoming officer resistance

Even though only officers with a demonstrated commitment to the program participated in Phase III, few of them believed that the program would lead to lower levels of violence among juveniles. Most felt that adolescents could obtain illegal firearms easily. Some acknowledged the possibility that the program could reduce youth violence if they got the "right" guns at the "right" time, but that prospect was considered unlikely, given the large pool of available firearms in a city with high levels of firearm violence.

What broke down the resistance of these Phase III officers was the return to working with the community, augmented by training and internal support. This led to an increased understanding of consent searches' deterrent effect.

What works

In Phase I, Consent-to-Search depended on city residents and organizations (block groups, Neighborhood Watch, parents) to determine which homes to search. Community-based selection of search targets seems to have secured greater cooperation and, ultimately, more guns. Perhaps residents have a more intuitive sense or better knowledge of which juveniles are likely to be harboring illegal guns.

However, the researchers believe that Phase III's more coordinated approach is the best model for this type of program because it enjoyed

greater support from police officers. Most officers saw value in such elements of the program as—

Problem solving. Officers valued using problem solving to address youth violence and other issues, especially assisting with non-law enforcement problems such as housing code violations, school problems, and unemployment.

Referral. Officers believed that the relatively modest crime-reduction effects of weapon seizure should have been complemented by other interventions. Frustrated by their inability to address underlying conditions, they appreciated having local clergy as community partners to whom they could refer parents and their children.

Deterrence. Many Phase III officers simply sought a safer community for youths. They were not as concerned with the target of the consent search—the guns—as they were with the message sent to parents and guardians in the community.

Intelligence gathering. Most officers felt that consent

Community-based selection of search targets seems to have secured greater cooperation and, ultimately, more guns.

searches provided an opportunity to gather information that otherwise would have been unavailable. They interacted more supportively with residents and observed the family circumstances of many juveniles.

Improved police image. Some officers hoped that residents would see them in a different light, more as partners than opponents. Although evaluators had no objective measure of this perception, they noted that some parents who were skeptical at the doorstep were cooperative by the end of the search.

For those seeking to implement gun recovery programs, Consent-to-Search sheds light on what works in this type of community policing response to gun violence if approaches from Phases I and III are combined:

- Use community sources to identify where to search.

- Place a higher priority on seizing guns than on prosecuting some young people.

- Emphasize deterrence and referral to social services.

- Train officers and ensure departmental support.

- Secure and maintain community participation and support.

- Establish procedures for recordkeeping and evaluation.

The Promise of Consent Searches

The consent search intervention has the potential to be part of a broader repertoire of tools the police can use to reduce firearms violence. Hundreds of guns were seized under the auspices of Consent-to-Search, and the police made many referrals to youth-serving agencies.

An irony of the Consent-to-Search program is the evaluators' finding that Phase III was more successful in the eyes of police officers than Phase I, despite lower gun recovery levels. Poorer results in Phase III may be mitigated by other factors. From the officers' viewpoint, more is at stake with this type of program than how many guns are taken. Convinced that seizing firearms alone does not adequately address youth gun violence, police preferred the community partnership and neighborhood targeting characteristics of Phase III. They also recognized the aggressive order maintenance and deterrent effects of searches, which sent a message to the community that illegal guns in the hands of juveniles will not be tolerated or ignored.[15]

Consent searches today

St. Louis still grapples with high rates of violence, especially homicide, aggravated assault, and robbery. In 2000, the city became a test site for a National Institute of Justice program called Strategic Approaches to Community Safety Initiative (SACSI). At each SACSI site, the U.S. Attorney, local decisionmakers, and a research partner collaborate to reduce crime. Researcher participation ensures that strategies will be based on real data, such as the finding that homicides in St. Louis are concentrated in 10 neighborhoods.

In 1998, St. Louis established a program based on the Boston model to address violent crime by focusing on the city's "hot spots." The program includes consent searches conducted by a trained team using the original tactics developed in 1993. The presence of a powerful external constituency—in this case, the U.S. Attorney—combined with police department support has helped integrate consent searches into routine policing. Teaming with community groups that have a stake in program success has completed the advocacy network needed to sustain the program.

In 2002, St. Louis became part of Project Safe Neighborhoods (PSN), a national initiative to reduce gun violence in America.[16] Like SACSI, Project Safe Neighborhoods fosters partnerships of Federal, State, and local law enforcement and community-based groups. One aspect is based on the premise that many youths are "career" offenders or victims (or both). Police follow up on emergency room gunshot and stab wound victims to prevent retaliatory violence and repeat victimization. Followup may include consent searches. Consent searches may also be integrated into another PSN program that will tackle gun violence in schools and among juveniles.

Thus, within the context of coordinated programs rooted in the community, consent searches have become a valuable element of a comprehensive gun violence reduction program.

A final observation

The Consent-to-Search experience shows that although problem-solving initiatives can be quite effective, they are relatively fragile. An innovative problem-solving intervention must rest on an established network of support among local justice professionals, elected officials, police leadership and field officers, and the community. The challenge is to sustain internal and external support for consent searches as part of a broader community mobilization to reduce firearms violence.

Notes

1. See Bryan, B., "Soft Sell of Searches Nets Police 3,900 Guns," *St. Louis Post-Dispatch,* April 10, 1995: 13a (hereinafter "Soft Sell of Searches").

2. Cook, P.J., and J.H. Laub, "The Unprecedented Epidemic in Youth Violence," in *Youth Violence,* vol. 24 of *Crime and Justice: A Review of Research,* ed. M. Tonry and M.H. Moore, Chicago: University of Chicago Press, 1998.

3. See Goldstein, H., "Improving Policing: A Problem-Oriented Approach," in *Thinking About Police: Contemporary Readings,* ed. C. Klockars and S. Mastrofski, New York: McGraw Hill, 1991; and Goldstein, H., *New Policing: Confronting Complexity,* Research in Brief, U.S. Department of Justice, National Institute of Justice, Washington, DC: 1993, NCJ 145157.

4. See Kennedy, D., "Pulling Levers: Getting Deterrence Right," *National Institute of Justice Journal* (July 1998): 2–8; and Kelling, G., and C. Coles, *Fixing Broken Windows: Restoring Order and Reducing Crime in Our Communities,* New York: Free Press, 1996.

5. The Consent-to-Search program's constitutionality was an issue for some local observers, but there are some legal precedents supporting this approach. Federal courts have ruled that the property of children can be searched with consent from their parents or guardians. For example, see *U.S.* v. *Rith,* 164 F.3d 1323 (10th Cir. 1999); and *U.S.* v. *Ladell,* 127 F.3d 622 (7th Cir. 1997).

6. Officers deliberately avoided confrontational or intimidating behavior. See Bryan, B., "Soft Sell of Searches." Also see Decker, S., and R. Rosenfeld, "From Problem Solving to Crime Suppression to Community Mobilization: An Evaluation of the St. Louis Consent-to-Search Program," final report, Washington, DC: U.S. Department of Justice, National Institute of Justice, 2001, NCJ 188291: 6. Available at http://www.ncjrs.org/pdffiles1/nij/grants/188291.pdf (hereinafter "From Problem Solving to Crime Suppression to Community Mobilization").

7. The U.S. Attorney heard about the Consent-to-Search program at a national conference and returned to St. Louis only to find that the idea had developed there years before. He used his leverage to ensure its reinstatement.

8. Funds were allocated from the Local Law Enforcement Block Grant, which also elevated the need for accountability—use of Federal funds to pay officer overtime to conduct consent searches required development of a system for reporting activity.

9. Because in many cases parents were absent or no one was home, results may underestimate the number of parents who might have permitted searches. See Decker, S., and R. Rosenfeld, "From Problem Solving to Crime Suppression to Community Mobilization": 15.

10. Ibid.: 8.

11. Ibid.: 12.

12. See Van Maanen, J., "Kinsmen in Repose: Occupational Perspectives of Patrolmen," in *The Police and Society: Touchstone Readings,* 2d ed., ed. V. Kappeler, Prospect Heights, IL: Waveland Press, 1999.

13. See Kennedy, D., A. Piehl, and A. Braga, "Youth Violence in Boston: Gun Markets, Serious Youth Offenders, and a Use-Reduction Strategy," *Law and Contemporary Problems* 59 (1996): 147–196; and Kennedy, D., A. Piehl, A. Braga, and E. Waring, *Reducing Gun Violence: The Boston Gun Project's Operation Ceasefire,* Research Report, Washington, DC: U.S. Department of Justice, National Institute of Justice, 2001, NCJ 188741.

14. See Sadd, S., and R.M. Grinc, *Implementation Challenges in Community Policing: Innovative Neighborhood-Oriented Policing in Eight Cities,* Research in Brief, Washington, DC: U.S. Department of Justice, National Institute of Justice, 1996, NCJ 157932.

15. Deterrence was also a critical factor in the Indianapolis Directed Patrol Project. See McGarrell, E.F., S. Chermak, and A. Weiss, *Reducing Gun Violence: Evaluation of the Indianapolis Police Department's Directed Patrol Project,* Research Report, Washington, DC: U.S. Department of Justice, National Institute of Justice, 2002, NCJ 188740.

16. For more information on Project Safe Neighborhoods, see http://www.psn.gov.

The National Institute of Justice is the
research, development, and evaluation
agency of the U.S. Department of Justice.
NIJ provides objective, independent,
evidence-based knowledge and tools
to enhance the administration
of justice and public safety.

NIJ is a component of the Office of Justice
Programs, which also includes the Bureau
of Justice Assistance, the Bureau of Justice
Statistics, the Office of Juvenile Justice
and Delinquency Prevention, and the
Office for Victims of Crime.